Concept Car

The cars of the future today

Concept cars are the very symbols of innovation and creativity. These cars are the wildest proposals of designers and engineers, mobile works of art that push the boundaries of technology and aesthetics. They are visions of the future, experimental models that pave new ways in the automotive industry.

Preface

But above all, concept cars are the expression of passion for cars, the desire to create something new, different, exciting. In this book, we will discover the most inspiring concept cars ever created and dive into the fascinating world of innovation and creativity in the automotive industry. Tomorrow is today.

Design is a fusion of aesthetics, functionality, and innovation that allows the creation of objects that enhance our daily lives. Concept cars are one of the most innovative forms of design in the automotive industry, created to explore new ideas, new materials, and new technologies.

Introduction

Concept cars may seem utopian, but they are in fact concrete projects, based on technology and creativity, that have the potential to transform our world. This book explores the links between design, concept cars, and utopia, offering a fascinating insight into the possible future of the automotive industry

Levanteo

Levanteo. This name is inspired by power and speed, evoking a fast and dynamic lifting movement. The name also suggests a certain elegance and sophistication, reminiscent of the distinctive style and high-end design of supercars.

Electric motor: 1.35 MW - 1810 Horsepower
*The total torque is 2,120 Nm, and the top speed of the **Levanteo** is 407 km/h. The 0 to 100 km/h is done in 2.01 seconds, and the 0 to 300 km/h in 9.7 seconds.*

Furya X.

Furya X. Fast, powerful, and aggressive with breathtaking performance. The "X" added at the end of the name brings this feeling of modernity, advanced technology, and innovation.

Electric motor: 1.48MW - 1984 Horsepower
*The total torque is 2,160 Nm, and the top speed of the **Furya X** is 416 km/h. The 0 to 100 km/h is done in 1.98 seconds, and the 0 to 300 km/h in 9.6 seconds.*

Aurora GT

*The **Aurora GT** shines like a northern light in the night. Elegant, obviously fast. Its velocity is as significant as its speed. The **Aurora GT** is a futuristic projection of cutting-edge technologies.*

Electric motor: 1.21MW - 1622 Horsepower
*The total torque is 1,899 Nm, and the top speed of the **Aurora GT** is 382 km/h. The 0 to 100 km/h is done in 2.31 seconds, and the 0 to 300 km/h in 10.7 seconds.*

Thunderbolt

The **Thunderbolt** is literally a thunderclap. Its aerodynamic design is inspired by lightning, with fluid and aggressive shapes that recall lightning in the sky. The car is equipped with a powerful electric motor that can deliver up to 1000 horsepower, propelling the car to a top speed of 400 km/h.

Electric motor: 0.747 MW - 1002 Horsepower
The top speed of the **Thunderbolt** is 403 km/h.

Electra

The **Electra** is capable of exceptional performance without using fossil fuel. The interior of the **Electra** is equipped with high-quality materials, with vegan leather seats and finishes in carbon fiber and aluminum. Advanced technologies such as high-definition touch screens and entertainment systems provide a personalized and immersive driving experience.

Electric motor: 0.75 MW - 999 Horsepower
The top speed of the **Electra** is 298 km/h. The 0 to 100 km/h is done in 2.9 seconds, and the 0 to 300 km/h in 11.3 seconds.

Invictus

The **Invictus** is first and foremost about strength and power. But it's also about resilience and determination. The Latin word "Invictus" means "invincible" or "indestructible", suggesting that this supercar is capable of overcoming all obstacles on the road.

Hydrogen motor: 1000 Horsepower
The top speed of the **Invictus** is 301 km/h.

Monarch 2030

*The **Monarch** symbolizes power and prestige. This exceptional car is capable of dominating the road. Its 2030 horsepower puts it at the top of this book. This **Monarch** recalls the brand's tradition of luxury and performance. With an elegant design and exceptional performance, the **Monarch** could become one of the most exclusive and coveted cars on the market.*

Electric motor: 1.514 MW - 2030 Horsepower.

Londoner GT

The **Londoner GT** pays tribute to the city of London and its chicest neighborhoods. It is equipped with a 6.0-liter bi-turbo V12 engine that delivers 700 horsepower and 800 Nm of torque. The design of the **Londoner GT** is inspired by iconic elements of London, with elegant lines and aerodynamic design elements that accentuate the car's performance.

Thermal engine: 711 Horsepower.

Xenith

Xenith evokes clarity and brilliance, and could symbolize for the brand the notions of seduction and modernity. The interior of the **Xenith** is luxurious and sophisticated, designed to provide maximum comfort to passengers.

Electric motor: 1.21MW - 1622 Horsepower.

Eosia

The name of the **Eosia** is derived from Eos, the Greek goddess of dawn, and evokes a sense of renewal and innovation. Aerodynamic design and lightweight materials such as carbon fiber for high top speed. The spacious and elegant cockpit would be equipped with the latest technology.

Hydrogen engine: 1985 Horsepower
The **Eosia** has a top speed of 406 km/h.

Equinox

*According to the designer, the name **Equinox** evokes balance and stability, suggesting that this supercar could be designed to offer a smooth and stable ride at high speeds. With an elegant design and advanced performance, the **Equinox** could become one of the most exclusive and sought-after supercars on the market in the future.*

Unknown engine.

Hydra

The **Hydra** is a futuristic sports car, powered by a hydrogen fuel cell that delivers exceptional performance while being environmentally friendly. The car's aerodynamic design is sleek and clean, with fluid curves and dynamic lines.

The **Hydra**'s hydrogen fuel cell system uses hydrogen stored in high-pressure tanks to produce electricity and power the electric motor. With its retro design, exceptional performance, and cutting-edge technology, the **Hydra** is the sports car of the future.

Unknown engine.

Carbon H2

*The **Carbone H2** is a cutting-edge supercar, powered by an advanced hydrogen fuel cell and built from carbon fiber. With blistering acceleration and exceptional handling, the car delivers an unforgettable driving experience. The interior is spacious and luxurious, with comfortable leather seats.*

Electric motorization: 1.447 MW - 1940 Horses
*The total torque is 2124 Nm, and the top speed of the **Carbone H2** is 423 km/h. The 0 to 100 km/h is done in 1.91 seconds, and the 0 to 300 km/h in 8.91 seconds.*

Hyperion

The **Hyperion** is designed to deliver exceptional performance and an unforgettable driving experience with an electric powertrain. The car's design is sleek and clean, with fluid curves and aggressive lines. The **Hyperion**'s electric system uses a high-performance battery to power the 4 electric motors. The car is equipped with advanced charging technologies for fast and efficient charging. The car can also be equipped with solar panels for an even more eco-friendly and economical recharge.

Unknown engine.

Viozela

*Sharp shapes designed to offer exceptional performance and a unique design. The name **Viozelia** is a combination of the words "violet" and "sensual," evoking the elegance, power, and beauty of this Concept Car. This vehicle is the very embodiment of audacity and sophistication.*

Thermal Engine: 950 Horsepower
V12 at 60°. Displacement 7,128 cm3, The total torque is 823 Nm at 6000 revolutions per minute.

Bianco

The **Bianco**, or, in reality, **Bianco Electra**, is a high-end electric supercar. The pure white color of the car adds a touch of sophistication to its bold and distinctive design. Exceptional performance, avant-garde design, and respect for the environment. With its unique combination of style, performance, and energy efficiency, this car will be a coveted addition to any high-end sports car collection.

Unknown engine.

Voltamante V1x

*The name **Voltamante V1x** is a combination of the words "volt" and "amante", evoking the electric power and passion for driving of this hypothetical endurance supercar. The car's design is optimized to minimize drag and maximize efficiency, with lines that do more than suggest speed and agility. The **Voltamante V1x** is an exceptional electric supercar designed for track endurance. With its unique combination of outstanding performance.*

Electric engine.

Phoenix

Phoenix evokes rebirth and renewal, suggesting that this exceptional vehicle capable of transporting 4 people represents a new era of 'family' sports cars. The 2 passenger seats have wood and aluminum finishes. With its 'small' V10 engine, the **Phoenix** is an exceptional supercar designed to combine cutting-edge performance, refined style, and luxurious comfort.

Thermal engine.

Murray M9

The **Murray M9** is a breathtaking supercar, with an aerodynamic and aggressive design inspired by the sleek and dynamic lines of a fighter jet. This car is equipped with a 5.2-liter V10 twin-turbo engine that produces an incredible power of over 900 horsepower. With a top speed of over 350 km/h, the **Murray M9** is one of the most promising cars.

Thermal engine: 900 Horsepower
V10 twin-turbo at 60°. Displacement 5,203 cm3, The total torque is 823 Nm at 5500 revolutions per minute.

Electra

The **Electra** is capable of exceptional performance without using fossil fuel.

The interior of the **Electra** is equipped with high-quality materials, including vegan leather seats and carbon fiber and aluminum finishes. Advanced technologies such as high-definition touchscreens and entertainment systems offer a personalized and immersive driving experience.

Electric powertrain: 0.75 MW - 999 Horsepower
The top speed of the **Electra** is 298 km/h. It accelerates from 0 to 100 km/h in 2.9 seconds and from 0 to 300 km/h in 11.3 seconds.

F9e Monte Carlo

The **F9e Monte Carlo** is at the intersection of three key aspects of supercars: Performance, Design, and Luxury. The figures are impressive and reflect the brutality of the beast.

A V12 engine, still the Holy Grail of the automotive world. The displacement is 6.3 liters, with a power output of 716 horsepower and a torque of 700 Nm.

The interior of the **F9e Monte Carlo** is luxurious, with red leather seats matching the car's bodywork, as well as carbon fiber and brushed aluminum finishes to enhance the sporty appearance.

Thermal engine: 716 Horsepower

The top speed of the **F9e Monte Carlo** is 342 km/h. It accelerates from 0 to 100 km/h in 3.4 seconds and from 0 to 300 km/h in 11.6 seconds.

Bellissimo Elegante

The **Bellissimo Elegante** offers an incredible driving experience. Its design is elegant and sophisticated, with a light blue metallic body that reflects light in a dazzling way. The curved lines and aerodynamic design elements enhance the car's performance and accentuate its Italian beauty. It is equipped with a 4.0-liter V8 twin-turbo engine that delivers 700 horsepower and a torque of 800 Nm. It can reach a top speed of over 330 km/h and go from 0 to 100 km/h in just 2.9 seconds.

Thermal engine: 700 Horsepower
The top speed of the **Bellissimo Elegante** is 330 km/h.

Dubaï Mirage

The **Dubai Mirage** is a mirage designed to drive between Sheikh Zayed Road and Al Satwa Road, ending the day on Al Maktoum Road in the heart of Dubai.

The design of the **Dubai Mirage** is inspired by the iconic architectural elements of Dubai, with clean lines.

It is equipped with a 6.0-liter V12 twin-turbo engine that delivers 900 horsepower and a torque of 1000 Nm.

Thermal engine: 900 Horsepower
The top speed of the **Dubai Mirage** is 380 km/h.

Voltara

*The **Voltara** is equipped with a high-performance electric propulsion system that delivers 600 horsepower and a torque of 700 Nm. It can reach a top speed of over 300 km/h and go from 0 to 100 km/h in just 3.6 seconds. The design of the **Voltara** is futuristic and dynamic, with fluid lines and aerodynamic design elements that enhance the car's performance.*

Electric engine: 0.445 MW – 602 Horsepower
*The top speed of the **Voltara** is 298 km/h. It accelerates from 0 to 100 km/h in 8.1 seconds.*

Aeroceano

The **Aeroceano** is a sleek and race-inspired car that offers an exceptional driving experience. It is equipped with a twin-turbo V12 engine that delivers 800 horsepower and a torque of 950 Nm.
The design of the **Aeroceano** is clean and aggressive, with aerodynamic lines and design elements that enhance the car's performance. The name **"Aeroceano"** evokes the combination of the power of air and sea, while the "GT" recalls the sporty and high-end aspect of the car.

Thermal engine: 800 Horsepower
The top speed of the **Aeroceano** is 350 km/h.
It accelerates from 0 to 100 km/h in 2.8 seconds.

Marco Silva

Marco Silva, 42 years old, is passionate about creating new forms and new experiences. His love for art and design led him to work in the automotive field, where he refined his sense of beauty and aesthetics. He offers an innovative approach and the ability to create designs that transcend norms and expectations. His style is recognizable by his unique blend of organic and geometric shapes, creating models that are both elegant and futuristic. His vision for the future of the automotive industry is fueled by an unwavering passion for innovation and excellence.

Made in United States
Orlando, FL
08 December 2024